Let's Hear It For

PIT BULLS

Precious McKenzie

rourkeeducationalmedia.com

*Scan for Related Titles
and Teacher Resources*

Before Reading:

Building Academic Vocabulary and Background Knowledge

Before reading a book, it is important to tap into what your child or students already know about the topic. This will help them develop their vocabulary, increase their reading comprehension, and make connections across the curriculum.

1. Look at the cover of the book. What will this book be about?
2. What do you already know about the topic?
3. Let's study the Table of Contents. What will you learn about in the book's chapters?
4. What would you like to learn about this topic? Do you think you might learn about it from this book? Why or why not?
5. Use a reading journal to write about your knowledge of this topic. Record what you already know about the topic and what you hope to learn about the topic.
6. Read the book.
7. In your reading journal, record what you learned about the topic and your response to the book.
8. After reading the book complete the activities below.

Content Area Vocabulary
Read the list. What do these words mean?

ancestry
companions
genetic
immigrants
mastiffs
prey
recognize
reputation
socialization
vermin

After Reading:

Comprehension and Extension Activity

After reading the book, work on the following questions with your child or students in order to check their level of reading comprehension and content mastery.

1. Why are some people afraid of pit bulls? (Summarize)
2. What traits make pit bulls such good fighters? (Infer)
3. How are the pit bull types alike? How are they different? (Asking questions)
4. Have you ever met a pit bull? Have you ever been afraid of a dog? (Text to self connection)
5. What are some of the ways people have mistreated animals? (Asking questions)

Extension Activity

After reading the book, pick one of the pit bull types. Do more research on that breed. Write a nonfiction report about the breed. Include photos or drawings that highlight that breed. Analyze the breed's characteristics and personality. Share your report with your class.

Table of Contents

Pit Bulls

When you hear "pit bull," do you imagine a fierce fighting dog? In the 1800s, people in Great Britain bred terriers, **mastiffs**, and bulldogs together. These early breeders wanted to create tough fighting dogs.

These dogs, the first pit bulls, were used in blood sports such as bull baiting and bear baiting. These cruel sports are now illegal in the United States and many other parts of the world.

The pit bull is a muscular, athletic dog with powerful jaws.

The term "pit bull" refers to types of dogs that were used to fight other animals, including other dogs, in pits.

Pit Bull Facts

Weight: 30-80 pounds (13-36 kilograms)

Height: 18-21 inches (45-54 centimeters)

Country of Origin: Great Britain

Life Span: 10-12 years

The American Kennel Club does not **recognize** pit bulls as a breed. Instead, "pit bull" is a general term used to describe at least five different breeds: the Bull Terrier, the American Bulldog, the Staffordshire Bull Terrier, the American Staffordshire Terrier, and the American Pit Bull Terrier.

Although the dogs share similarities, they also have their differences. Many people have difficulty telling the pit bull types of dogs apart.

Bull Terrier

American Bulldog

In 2004, the New York City Animal Care and Control tried to rename pit bulls "New Yorkies."

"New Yorkers, like pit bulls, are sometimes perceived as a standoffish and mean breed—but are actually some of the most generous and open-hearted people I've ever met," animal control director Ed Boks said.

American Pit Bull Terrier

Staffordshire Bull Terrier

American Staffordshire Terrier

The Breeds

Bull Terrier

In the 1800s, breeders mated the White English Terrier with the bulldog to create the Bull Terrier. They used the Bull Terrier in dog fights, bull baiting, and to hunt **vermin**.

By 1835, blood sports such as bull baiting were outlawed in England.

Bull Terriers are about 20 inches (48 centimeters) tall. They are muscular and solid.

Today, Bull Terriers are delightful family **companions**. Bull Terriers are loyal to their people and love to play. Bull Terrier owners describe them as clown-like.

Bull Terriers are medium-sized dogs, weighing about 45 pounds (20.5 kilograms).

American Bulldog

Like the Bull Terrier, the American Bulldog had its beginnings in England. It was used to guard property, drive cattle, and hunt small game. **Immigrants** brought these dogs to the United States.

The American Bulldog weighs between 75 and 100 pounds (34-45 kilograms). They are about 25 inches (64 centimeters) tall.

By World War II, the breed almost vanished until John D. Johnson and Allen Scott created a new breeding program. The American Bulldog would be extinct if they hadn't!

When bull baiting and other blood sports were outlawed in England, people developed other smaller dogs such as the English Bulldog.

English Bulldog

The American Bulldog needs work to do. It is athletic, strong, and is a natural guardian. They are not afraid of intruders and will defend their family, no matter what.

Staffordshire Bull Terrier

Though it's part of the terrier group, the Staffordshire Bull Terrier shares **ancestry** with the other pit bull types of dogs. Similar to other terriers, the Staffordshire Bull Terrier has an intense **prey** drive and is prized as a vermin catcher.

Staffordshire Bull Terriers are about 14-16 inches (35-41 centimeters) tall and weigh between 24-38 pounds (10-17 kilograms).

The Staffordshire Bull Terrier is stubborn and curious. Although it loves people, Staffordshire Bull Terrier breeders recommend firm, strong training. This dog needs to know you are the leader.

American Staffordshire Terrier

Breeders in the United States wanted a stronger, heavier dog than the Staffordshire Bull Terrier. They developed the American Staffordshire Terrier, or AmStaff. A close cousin to the Staffordshire Bull Terrier, the American Staffordshire Terrier is heavier than the Staffordshire Bull Terrier, and just as courageous.

AmStaffs are heavy dogs. They usually weigh between 62-88 pounds (28-40 kilograms).

The AmStaff is stocky, muscular, quick, and graceful. They need games and training to stay alert and challenged, or they get bored and might get into trouble.

The American Pit Bull Terrier

The American Pit Bull Terrier is not considered an official purebred dog by the American Kennel Club. However, the United Kennel Club does consider the American Pit Bull Terrier as its own breed. The American Pit Bull Terrier shares the same history as the other pit bulls. But some historians think that pit dogs from Ireland and Scotland were also used in the early development of this breed.

American Pit Bull Terriers are about 20 inches (50 centimeters) tall. They weigh between 30-65 pounds (13-29 kilograms).

Is the Staffordshire Terrier the same as the American Pit Bull Terrier or not? Breeders and kennel clubs can't reach an agreement. It will probably take many more years of **genetic** studies and careful breeding to determine if the American Pit Bull Terrier is a breed of its own.

Some Staffordshire Terriers are also registered as American Pit Bull Terriers.

Like most dogs, American Pit Bull Terriers need exercise and play to stay healthy.

Proper Training

All of the pit bull types of dogs are closely related and share a common history. Unfortunately, their history is one of combat.

Pit bulls still have a **reputation** as killers.

That's because of an increase in illegal dog fighting cases in the United States. Dog fight promoters use pit bulls because of their courage and strength.

It is illegal to stage dog fights for entertainment or profit, but it still happens.

Any dog is capable of biting or attacking. Each dog is an individual. Firm, loving training and early **socialization** is the best plan for each and every dog, not just pit bulls.

Pit bulls may have a reputation as fighting machines, but well-trained pit bulls can be delightful, protective companions.

From 1982 - 2014, in Canada and the United States, pit bulls were responsible for the deaths of 295 people.

Doggie Advice

Puppies are cute and cuddly but buying one should never be done without serious thought. Choosing the right breed of dog requires some homework. And remember that a dog will require more than love and great patience. It will require food, exercise, a warm, safe place to live, and medical care.

A dog can be your best friend, but you need to be its best friend, too. For more information about buying and owning a dog, contact the American Kennel Club at www.akc.org/index.cfm or the Canadian Kennel Club at www.ckc.ca.

Glossary

ancestry (an-SESS-tree): members of the same family who lived in the past

companions (kuhm-PAN-yuhnz): friends who you spend time with

genetic (juh-NET-ik): study of how traits are passed from one generation to the next

immigrants (IM-uh-gruhntss): people who moved from faraway to live in a new land

mastiffs (MASS-tifss): some of the largest dogs in the world

prey (PRAY): an animal that is hunted by another

recognize (REK-uhg-nize): to see, understand, or know

reputation (rep-yuh-TAY-shuhn): one's character

socialization (SOH-shuh-liz-AY-shuhn): early training around others

vermin (VUR-min): small rodents and harmful pests

Index

Show What You Know

1. What were early pit bulls used for in Great Britain?
2. What characteristics do most pit bull types have in common?
3. How should dogs be trained?

Websites to Visit

www.akc.org
www.loveyourdog.com
http://americanbulldogrescue.org

About the Author

Precious McKenzie lives in Montana with her three furry and friendly hounds. The most recent addition to her family is a retired racing greyhound. They love to take long walks, play with tennis balls for hours, and chase rabbits.

Meet The Author!
www.meetREMauthors.com

PHOTO CREDITS: Cover and page 7 bottom right © Eponaleah; pages 4-5 © tomas devera photo, inset photo page 5 © Jenn_C; page 6 bottom left © otsphoto, bottom right © Dominik Michalowski, page 7 bottom left © Richard Chaff, bottom right © Vera Zinkova; page 8 © Ksenia Merenkova, page 9 top © Rita Kochmarjova, bottom © otsphoto; page 10 © Erik Lam, page 11 top © Best dog photo, bottom © Melounix; page 12 © cynoclub, page 13 top © Erik Lam, bottom © PolinaBright; page 14 © cynoclub, page 15 top © Eric Isselee, bottom © Grisha Bruev; page 16 © Thirdparty, page 17 © Janis Smits; page 18-19 © cynoclub, page 19 © DreamBig; page 20 © Djem, page 21 © Alena Kazlouskaya. All photos from Shutterstock.com

Edited by: Keli Sipperley

Cover design and layout: Nicola Stratford   www.nicolastratford.com

Library of Congress PCN Data

Let's Hear It For Pit Bulls / Precious McKenzie
(Dog Applause)
ISBN 978-1-68342-167-2 (hard cover)
ISBN 978-1-68342-235-8 (e-Book)
Library of Congress Control Number: 2016956594

Also Available as:
ROURKE'S
e-Books

Printed in the United States of America, North Mankato, Minnesota

24

The Animal Kingdom

ANIMAL SIGNALS

Malcolm Penny

Illustrated by Carolyn Scrace

The Bookwright Press
New York · 1989

The Animal Kingdom

Animal Adaptations
Animal Camouflage
Animal Defenses
Animal Evolution
Animal Homes
Animal Migration
Animal Movement

Animal Partnerships
Animal Reproduction
Animal Signals
Animals and their Young
Endangered Animals
The Food Chain
Hunting and Stalking

First published in the
United States in 1989 by
The Bookwright Press
387 Park Avenue South
New York, NY 10016

First published in 1988 by
Wayland (Publishers) Ltd
61 Western Road, Hove
East Sussex BN3 1JD, England

Library of Congress Cataloging-in-Publication Data

Penny, Malcolm
   Animal signals / by Malcolm Penny: [Illustrated by Carolyn Scrace].
      p. cm.—(The animal kingdom)
   Bibliography: p.
   Includes index.
   Summary. Describes the various ways in which animals communicate
with each other for such purposes as mating, challenges, and friendship.
   ISBN 0–531–18224–X
   1. Animal communication—Juvenile literature. [1. Animal communication.]
I. Scrace, Carolyn, ill. II. Title. III. Series: Penny, Malcolm. Animal kingdom.
QL776.P46 1989
591.59—dc19

88–14466
CIP
AC

Typeset by DP Press, Sevenoaks, Kent, England
Printed by Casterman SA, Belgium

Words printed in **bold** in the text
are explained in the glossary on page 30.

Contents

Animal language

Visual signals *Brimstone butterflies use color to signal to one another that they are either male or female.*

Sound signals *Red deer stags roar during the breeding season to show off their strength.*

Scent signals *Otters mark their territory by leaving piles of strong-smelling spraint.*

Touch signals *Male and female giraffes are sometimes seen "necking."*

Almost all animals pass messages to each other by means of signals. The signals may be something the animals can see – these are called visual signals – or they may be in the form of scent, sound, or touch. Signals can have many meanings. Some of them are warnings to other animals or signs of **surrender**. Others are invitations to another animal to mate and produce young – these are called **courtship** signals. Young animals may use signals to ask for food or protection from their parents.

We can never really talk with animals, or fully understand their signals, but by watching them closely, we can figure out what some of the signals mean, and even teach animals to respond to some of the signals we make to them.

Sound signals
Red deer stag

Female

Visual signals
Brimstone butterflies

Male

Scent signals
Otters

Touch sign

Dogs that live with people soon learn to exchange signals with them. Some of a dog's signals are the same ones it would use to pass a message to another dog; for example, growling and showing its teeth or wagging its tail. Others are meant only for people: a dog would not take its leash or its feeding bowl to another dog, but only to its owner.

We can teach the dog to obey certain commands, from simple instructions like sitting still to complicated activities like rounding up sheep or helping a blind person to move around.

All these signals have several things in common. They are made using sounds or movements natural to the signaler. For example, a dog may signal by barking and a human by whistling, but it would not happen the other way around. Each has a purpose, which is to exchange information. Also, a signal has to be learned, by both the animal giving it and the animal receiving it. In this book, we shall look at many of the signals animals make to one another.

In the Galapagos Islands a male and female waved albatross perform a beak-clapping display to each other as part of their courtship. Each bird constantly signals to reduce the other bird's aggression, so that they will be able to mate.

Fine feathers and special nests

The courtship signals that birds make to each other are easy to see, and many of them seem to have obvious meanings. Male birds with spectacular **plumage**, such as peacocks and birds of paradise, show off their feathers to females in what are called displays. The fine feathers show how big and strong the bird is. A female is attracted to a well-fed, colorful male because he is likely to be the father of healthy chicks.

Some birds show off by other means. Male weaver finches of Africa build nests before they begin to **court** a female. When the nest is nearly finished, the male hangs upside down underneath it, fluttering his wings and calling. Soon a female will come to inspect the nest, to see whether it is the place where she wants to lay her eggs.

Head-shaking

Weed dance

Inviting pose

Male black-hooded weaver finches weaving grass nests.

Male frigate birds can inflate their throat pouches like giant red balloons. This signals to females that they are ready to mate.

Above left *Great-crested grebes use many different displays during courtship, including the three shown above. Each of the displays has its own special meaning. When the pair of birds have performed all the rituals, and have received all the signals, they are ready to mate.*

In Australia, male bower birds use grass to build a chamber, which is then decorated with small, bright objects. The bird places the objects as a trail, which the female follows until she enters the courtship chamber or bower. Once, bower birds used only flowers, feathers and small pebbles to decorate the chamber, but now they often use broken glass and the shiny metal tops of drink cans.

Birds of the grouse family use a much bigger courtship area. The males gather together to display in a group to attract females. Such gatherings are called leks, and the lekking grounds are used year after year by particular groups of birds.

The song of birds has puzzled people for centuries. Because humans usually sing when they are happy, it is tempting to think that the birds are happy too, but this is not the meaning of birdsong. Sometimes a male is calling for a female to come and be his mate, but more often he is warning other males not to come near him. We shall find out more about birdsongs in chapters seven and eleven.

Courtship in mammals

The courtship signals between **mammals** are different from those used by birds. Mammals are not so colorful as birds and so must show off in another way. Many male mammals have fine horns or antlers that may be used for fighting, but more often they are there for show. This is not so much to attract females as to drive away other males.

Animals such as elk or mountain goats have such strong, sharp horns that fighting is dangerous for both the animals involved. The same is true of rhinoceroses and other animals with horns. If they fight at all, it is in a careful way called **sparring**.

More often, these animals settle their differences by making threatening signals. They may bellow or roar loudly, as red deer **stags** do, or they may pretend to charge, giving their rivals a chance to escape, as rhinoceroses often do. When only one male is left, he will be able to court any females that have been attracted by the sounds of the contest.

Other animals call to each other in order to find a mate. The cat family is well known for this, especially domestic cats, which may keep the whole neighborhood awake when they call at night!

Scent is a very important way of signaling among mammals. When a female mammal is in season, which means that her **eggs** are ready to be **fertilized**, she begins to smell different. The scent she produces is a powerful signal to males of the same species, telling them she is ready to mate.

Some mammals use visual signals to show that they are ready to mate. Female baboons develop bright colors on their rumps and faces to attract males of their own species. Male mandrills have very bright rumps and facial markings to signal their strength to one another and to females.

In Western Africa a brightly colored male mandrill signals his power to a female behind him. In the background a male drill signals his aggression to two other drills by shrieking.

8

Calling frogs and dancing fish

Although fish can use sound and scent as a way of signaling, they use mostly visual signals including bright colors and graceful movements, to attract a mate. Sticklebacks, which are found in northern fresh waters and sea inlets, are a very good example.

A male stickleback begins by making a nest, which is a tube of pieces of pondweed stuck into a hollow on the bottom of the pond. He then performs a zig-zag dance toward any female that comes near the nest, until she follows him down to swim into it. She is attracted by his bright red and silver colors, as well as by the way in which he moves. If another red male comes too near his nest, the male stickleback will attack him very fiercely until he goes away.

Amphibians include newts, frogs and toads. Newts use a variety of courtship signals. Some of them are visual, like the stickleback's dance, but often they signal by scent, which the male wafts through the water toward the female with his tail.

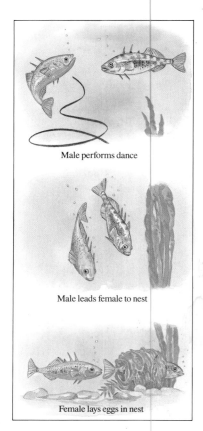

Male performs dance

Male leads female to nest

Female lays eggs in nest

Above *In his breeding colors, a male stickleback dances to attract a female. He leads her to the nest, where they will breed.*

Left *The beautiful markings of the male mandarin fish act as a visual signal to the female, attracting her to mate with him. These fish are found in warm tropical waters.*

A male painted reed frog calls to attract a mate at night in southern Africa.

Frogs and toads use sound as a way of calling their mates to them. In **tropical rain forests**, where there are many different species of frogs, each has its own call, ranging from the deep croaks of bullfrogs to high-pitched chirrups and whistles produced by small tree frogs.

Snakes cannot signal to each other with sounds because they are deaf. Instead, they use scent to attract a mate, and color to recognize their own **species**. When a pair is close enough together, they use touch as the final stage of courtship, often winding around each other as they mate.

Lizards use mostly visual signals to attract their mates. The anole lizards of North and South America are among the most spectacular. Below their throats the males have flaps of brightly colored skin, which they can flip in and out to make a very obvious signal.

Courtship signals of invertebrates

Insects and spiders are invertebrates, which means animals without backbones. They signal to one another mainly by scent and sight, although sound is important to some of them.

Female moths use scent to attract males from far away when they are ready to breed. The male detects the scent with his **antennae**, always flying in the direction of the scent until he finds the female.

Butterflies use scent differently. Unlike moths, they fly during the day, so males and females find each other using visual signals, such as the colors and patterns on their wings. However, some different species of butterfly have such similar patterns that it is possible to make a mistake. Therefore, the male often uses scent to make sure the female is the right species. If she is of a different species, she will not respond to his scent signal.

Below *A male garden spider (the smaller) treads carefully as he approaches the much larger female to mate with her. He must be careful to signal correctly or she may eat him instead!*

Left *A glow-worm photographed at dusk. As the beetle waves its abdomen to and fro, it produces a flashing yellow light to attract a mate.*

Crickets and grasshoppers use sound signals. The males call and the females come to find them, often choosing the males that make the loudest calls.

The brightest visual signal is produced by glow-worms and fireflies, both of which are actually beetles. Their bodies glow a bright green in the dark, which helps the males and females to find each other for mating.

Spiders use a wide range of signals. Some of them are visual. An example is the **semaphore** of the wolf spider, which waves its **palps**, shaped like boxing gloves. Spiders that build webs use signals that involve the male's twanging the strands of the web so that the female can feel the **vibrations**. He has to be careful because certain types of vibrations are a sign to the female that an insect has been caught in her web. If the male gets his signal wrong, she might eat him instead of mating with him!

Below *Wolf spiders signal to one another by waving their heavy palps.*

13

Signals within the family

When parents call to their children, or animals call to each other as they move around, they are said to be making "contact calls." This is how they keep in touch, so that each knows where the other is. Many of the sounds made by flocks of birds are for this purpose.

Some of the family signals are more urgent. When a mother duck calls her young to follow her, they must obey at once because the call may be to save them from danger. When they first leave the nest, they must also follow their mother's call. This can lead them into a frightening situation – many ducks nest in trees or even on high buildings, and the babies must jump to the ground. However, their mother knows how to lead them to safety and the ducklings are well protected by their soft down.

Ring-tailed lemurs in Madagascar use several signals to keep the troop together. Before they set off through the forest, the adults give a series of clicking calls so that the younger lemurs know that it is time to move. Older animals show their importance within the group in an unusual way. They rub their tails between their wrists, covering the tails with scent from special **glands**. Then they flick the tails over their heads to spread the scent through the air. The tails themselves act as signals: they are long and fluffy, marked with black and white bands, and are very easy to follow in the shady forest.

Bees, wasps and ants use scent signals to keep the swarm together. Scents produced by the **queen** are passed from one **worker** to another. The scent works in two ways: it enables the workers to recognize one another, and it controls their actions, so that each knows when more food is needed, or when there are young to look after.

Opposite In a tropical forest on Madagascar, a tribe of ring-tailed lemurs signal to one another with their tails. The lemur in the foreground is scent-marking his tail using scent glands on his wrists.

14

Keeping a territory

On the African plains a male rhinoceros squirts urine to mark his territory. The pile of dung on the ground is another territorial signal. On the left, a dik-dik rubs its scent gland on a bush to mark its territory. Neither of these animals can understand the other's signal because they are different species.

When a male bird sings, it is usually defending its territory. This is an area taken over by the bird from which it will drive away all other males of its own species. The song is a warning that this particular area is occupied. An animal needs its territory to provide enough food for its mate and their young, and often to keep its mate from being taken away by other males.

Animal territories can be small or very large. The territory of a speckled wood butterfly may be less than a square inch of sunlight on a fern leaf, while a male white rhinoceros on the African plains must defend a territory of several square miles.

Animals use many different signals to warn off others from their territory. The rhinoceros sprays **urine** and leaves piles of dung around the borders of his territory, so that other rhinos know they should not enter this area.

Dogs and lions also use urine to mark places within their hunting range. Otters leave strongly scented dung called spraint in open places along their own stretches of river bank.

Many animals have special scent glands, which they use for marking territory. Male rabbits use scent glands under their chins, while antelope such as the dik-dik of southern Africa use scent glands on their cheeks.

Birds use their colors as an important visual signal for defending their territory. Many breeding birds, especially those of dark forests, are brightly colored when they are breeding, so that their rivals can see them and avoid the danger of a fight.

Seabirds such as gulls and cormorants, which nest in crowded **colonies**, defend very small territories consisting of a narrow space around each nest. To reduce fighting, the birds use signals to warn rivals away. Because the breeding colonies are very noisy, the birds make visual signals, moving their heads, bodies and wings in certain ways.

Threat signals

Animals may threaten their own kind, as males do during the courtship period, or they may threaten animals of other species. Some signals work in both situations: when a dog bares its teeth and growls, the signal means the same whether it is signaling to another dog, to a horse or to a human being. The same is true of a cat, arching its back and hissing – the message is unmistakable.

We do not usually think of rabbits as being threatening animals, but they may need to threaten each other. Sometimes they simply run toward a rival; at other times they seem to feed quietly, but are in fact moving toward him. An intruder will understand at once that he is being threatened, and move away. Sometimes a male rabbit begins to scratch the ground with his front feet, or to move on tiptoe with stiff legs, or even to squirt urine at his rival. These are serious threats, and other rabbits would be well advised to get out of the way at once.

Below left *A young kitten hisses threateningly as it sees a spider for the first time. Of course, the spider does not understand this signal. Notice that the kitten's hair is standing on end, which shows fright or alarm.*

Below right *When the American rattlesnake shakes its rattle, it is a clear signal to other animals to keep away.*

Wild dogs use many of the signals that we see in pet dogs. When they wish to threaten each other, they can also use signals that are less obvious, as if they were a secret code between dogs. A dog standing quite still, with its head up and its ears pricked, but its tail hanging still is actually showing the beginning of a threat. If its rival does not move away, there might well be a fight.

Some animals give signals that their own species cannot possibly receive. Rattlesnakes are the perfect example: the rattle cannot be heard by other snakes, but it acts as an important signal to other animals, and this may save two lives at once. It warns approaching large animals not to tread on the snake, thus saving the rattlesnake from a serious injury and at the same time saving the large animal from suffering a poisonous bite.

Two male Cape hunting dogs threaten each other. The posture of the dog on the left is mildly threatening, while the dog on the right is snarling very aggressively.

Signals of surrender

When an animal is threatened, it can either run away or stay where it is. If it wishes to stay but not to fight, it must give a signal of surrender.

When a wild dog surrenders to a senior dog in the pack, it whines quietly, draws back its lips without showing its teeth, lowers its head and crouches to the ground, wagging its tail. All these signals make it look small and defenseless, like a puppy. Even its whining makes it sound like a baby. Older dogs would never harm a puppy, so they leave it alone.

Signals of this kind are found throughout the animal kingdom. When an adult bird flutters its wings to another adult, it is **imitating** a harmless baby. When a young male elephant seal creeps into the territory of a much bigger bull seal, it pulls its trunk in. It is not pretending to be a baby

A male Arctic tern offers a gift of a sand eel to the female during their courtship. She is sitting in a submissive posture to receive the gift, so as not to threaten the male. These birds breed in northern countries around the Arctic Circle.

– it is far too large for that – but instead it is trying to look like a female, offering no challenge to the big bull. If the bull knew it was a male, the youngster would be attacked and probably badly hurt.

Some male fish, especially those that live on coral reefs or in the great freshwater lakes of Africa, actually change color to look like a female if there is a more powerful male nearby.

Another signal of surrender, with which many animals end a fight, is for the loser to offer the winner the chance to hurt or even kill it. Most animals try to end a fight as quickly as possible. Instead of trying to kill the loser, which might fight back, the winner moves away. All kinds of dogs, from coyotes in the United States and Canada to dingoes in Australia, show their throats or bellies when they know there is no point in fighting on.

If a young male elephant seal does not give the correct signals of submission, an older male may challenge him. The photograph shows two males fighting in South Georgia, an island in the South Atlantic Ocean.

Danger signals

Animals living in groups that are likely to be attacked by a passing **predator** need ways of warning one another of the approach of danger.

Prairie dogs in the United States and Canada make a high-pitched whistle if they see an eagle or a mountain lion. The signal sends all other prairie dogs scurrying for the safety of their burrows.

Kangaroos and rabbits thump the ground and run for cover. As rabbits run to their burrows they give a visual signal as well, by turning their tails up to show the white underside. Many deer do the same with their tails. The sight of white tails bobbing up and down as their owners run away makes other animals want to run as well.

Meerkats are a kind of mongoose that live in Namibia, Africa. They often stand on guard like this. The first one to see or hear danger calls to the others, warning them to run to safety.

Flocks of birds warn of danger using visual and sound signals. When a goose or a shore bird, such as a plover or a sandpiper, suddenly takes to the air, all the other members of the flock take off as well. When one bird gives the danger call, all the birds in the area will fly away, no matter which species gives the call.

People make use of some birds' warning calls. The danger calls of gulls are often played very loudly from tape recorders at airports to keep birds away from the runways. If gulls were sucked into an airplane's jet engine, they could cause a crash.

Many mammals react to any warning signal, as if it were from their own species. In India, swamp deer bark as soon as they smell or see a tiger. At once, all the other deer nearby, including sambur and chital, look up and move away from the danger. All Indian animals will pay attention if they hear a peacock calling at night in the forest. They have learned that peacocks call when they see a tiger.

In India a swamp deer barks as she notices a tiger stalking her. This alarm signal warns the other swamp deer and a chital to run for their lives.

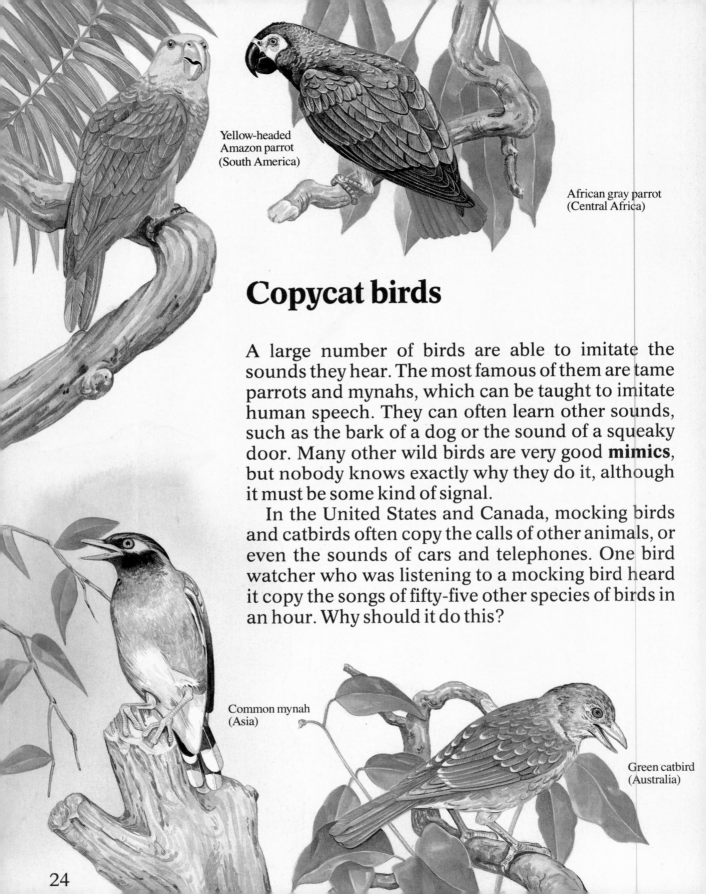

Yellow-headed
Amazon parrot
(South America)

African gray parrot
(Central Africa)

Copycat birds

A large number of birds are able to imitate the sounds they hear. The most famous of them are tame parrots and mynahs, which can be taught to imitate human speech. They can often learn other sounds, such as the bark of a dog or the sound of a squeaky door. Many other wild birds are very good **mimics**, but nobody knows exactly why they do it, although it must be some kind of signal.

In the United States and Canada, mocking birds and catbirds often copy the calls of other animals, or even the sounds of cars and telephones. One bird watcher who was listening to a mocking bird heard it copy the songs of fifty-five other species of birds in an hour. Why should it do this?

Common mynah
(Asia)

Green catbird
(Australia)

Mocking bird
(USA)

Many birds use songs instead of fine feathers as a way of attracting a mate. Perhaps for some species of birds a very complicated song is the best way to attract a mate. It could be that a mocking bird's extremely complicated song works in the same way as a peacock's beautiful feathers.

Some people say that birds mimic other animals that prey on them, to drive the predator away. The British jay is sometimes attacked by tawny owls. When this happens it hoots like an owl.

In Australia, a bird called the bushlark imitates other birds while it is flying. An even better mimic in Australia and New Zealand is the British starling, which was introduced to these countries in the last century. It has learned to copy the calls, not only of other birds from Britain, like blackbirds, but also those of local Australian and New Zealand birds.

Jay (Europe)

Starling
(Europe, North America, Australia)

The birds illustrated on this page all mimic other birds' songs. They do this for many different reasons.

The mysterious sound signals of whales

In the past, sailors in wooden sailing ships often said that they had heard strange songs coming from under the water, especially when they were lying in their bunks on a calm night. They used to think that they were the songs of mermaids. About twenty-five years ago, an American scientist, Dr. Roger Payne, began to record these strange and beautiful songs from under the sea. These songs were the calls of humpback whales.

Dr. Payne found that all the whales sang very similar songs, which changed a little from year to year. Sound travels very quickly under water, so whales can hear one another even if they are many miles apart. There are several records of these songs, which people can buy to listen to at home, but no one has ever discovered what they mean.

Like all whales, narwhals signal to one another using a complex range of different sounds. These creatures live in the Arctic Ocean, and once people thought that the males were unicorns because of their long tusks.

Since then, scientists have recorded the sounds of killer whales, which make many different noises. Some of the sounds are clicks, which help the whale to find its prey, rather like the whistles and buzzes of bats and swifts. Others are more like squeaks and grunts. Again, nobody knows what they mean, but the strange thing is that all the killer whales in one family use one set of about twelve sounds, and other families use different sets, as if they speak in a different language.

Recordings with underwater microphones have now been made of every species of whale, and many dolphins. Some of the calls are much simpler than those of the humpback and the killer whale, but they must all mean something to other whales of the right species.

Whales live in such a different world from ours that we may never understand their sounds. What is clear is that they are very intelligent creatures and can understand very complicated signals.

Dolphins whistle and squeak to each other and also to humans, although we do not understand many of their signals.

How animals signal to people

Parrots and mynahs may make sounds that humans can understand, but they are not true signals because the bird is not using them to pass on information. Dogs and cats can tell us things by their signals. When a dog presents us with a stick or a cat scratches at the door, we know what they want.

Wild animals can signal certain things to people. Sometimes people who are snorkeling on a coral reef are attacked by tiny fish, which are warning them to keep away from their eggs. Large birds such as trumpeter swans in Canada, or eagles all over the world, will attack people who approach their nests. These signals are obvious and easy to understand, but they are not a language.

Recently, scientists have been trying to teach animals to use language in the form of more complicated signals that people can understand.

The facial expressions of chimpanzees reveal many different moods. Humans have been able to understand some of their expressions, as the illustration shows.

Greeting pout

Excitement or fear

Contentment or playfulness

Threatening

Koko the gorilla with her second pet kitten, photographed in 1985 at the Gorilla Foundation of California. You can see how much Koko cares for her tiny pet.

Dogs often signal to their owners that they would like to play or go for a walk.

Chimpanzees and gorillas seem to be the best at learning. One famous gorilla called Koko was able to signal to her trainers when she wanted food or a ball to play with, even though she could not see the food or the ball. Koko had a pet kitten, and she was very upset when the kitten died. Her trainers brought her a new one, but she told them in sign language that it was not the same as the old one.

However, even Koko could signal only a few simple things to her trainers. She could no doubt pass on much more information to another gorilla. It may be more important, as well as more interesting, for humans to learn about the signals that wild gorillas, and all kinds of other animals, make to one another.

Glossary

Amphibians Cold-blooded animals that live on land but breed in water. Frogs, toads, newts and salamanders are all amphibians.

Antennae The pair of "feelers" on an insect's head, sometimes used for passing on a signal.

Colonies Groups of one species of animal that live together.

Court To try to attract a female for the purpose of mating.

Courtship The process during which male and female animals signal to each other that they are looking for a mate.

Eggs The sex cells produced by female animals.

Fertilized Made ready to develop into a new creature. When a female's egg is fertilized, by joining with a male's sperm, it can begin to grow into a baby.

Glands Organs in an animal's body that produce a particular substance, such as sweat or poison.

Imitate To copy the sounds made by another animal.

Mammals Warm-blooded animals, usually having hairy skin, whose females feed their young with milk.

Mimic An animal that copies the sound, and sometimes the appearance, of another animal.

Palps Feelers around a spider's mouth.

Plumage The often very colorful feathers that birds may use for displays.

Predator An animal that hunts other animals for food.

Queen The ruling female in a colony of bees, wasps or ants. Only the queens can mate with the males and produce all the young.

Semaphore To signal by moving the limbs. Humans semaphore with their arms.

Sparring A kind of fighting that usually does not lead to either animal's being badly hurt.

Species A group of animals or plants that is different from all other groups.

Stag The word for an adult male deer.

Surrender To give in to a stronger animal.

Tropical rain forests Dense, moist forests found in tropical parts of the world where there is heavy rainfall. Rain forests contain millions of species of animals and plants.

Urine The pale yellow liquid produced by the kidneys, stored in the bladder and discharged from the body as waste.

Vibrations Movements that can be felt.

Worker A female insect, usually a bee, a wasp or an ant, that cannot lay eggs but looks after the babies of other females.

Picture acknowledgments

The photographs in this book were taken by: Bruce Coleman Limited 5 and 22 (Gunter Ziesler), 10 (Jane Burton), 13 (Peter Hinchliffe); Oxford Scientific Films 11 (Michael Fogden); Popperfoto 29 (Reuter); Survival Anglia Limited 7 (Alan Root), 18 (Jeff Foott), 21 (Annie Price).

Further information

To find out more about how animals signal to one another, you may wish to read the books suggested below:

Animal Defenses by Malcolm Penny. The Bookwright Press, 1988.

Animal Sounds by Golden Books, Aurelius Battaglia, illustrator. Western Publishing Co., 1981.

Bird Talk by Roma Gans. Crowell Jr. Books, 1971.

Discovering Butterflies and Moths by Keith Porter. The Bookwright Press, 1986.

Discovering Crabs and Lobsters by Jill Bailey. The Bookwright Press, 1987.

Discovering Snakes and Lizards by Neil Curtis. The Bookwright Press, 1985.

Discovering Spiders by Malcolm Penny. The Bookwright Press, 1985.

Gobble, Growl, Grunt by Peter Spier. Doubleday and Co., 1971.

There are some excellent wildlife films on television that often show animals using signals. You can learn more about wild animals, and help to protect them, by joining one of the organizations listed below:

**Audubon Naturalist Society
  of the Central Atlantic States**
8940 Jones Mill Road
Chevy Chase, Maryland 20815

The Conservation Foundation
1717 Massachusetts Avenue, N.W.
Washington, D.C. 20036

Greenpeace
1611 Connecticut Avenue, N.W.
Washington, D.C. 20009

The Humane Society of the USA
2100 L Street, N.W.
Washington, D.C. 20037

**The International Fund
  for Animal Welfare**
P.O. Box 193
Yarmouth Port, Massachusetts 02675

National Wildlife Federation
1412 16th Street, N.W.
Washington, D.C. 20036

The World Wildlife Fund
1255 23d Street, N.W.
Washington, D.C. 20037

Index

32